Warriors with Broken Pieces

Helaina Brunel

BookLeaf Publishing

India | USA | UK

Presentation by *BookLeaf Publishing*

Web: www.bookleafpub.com

E-mail: info@bookleafpub.com

ISBN : 9789357448987

First edition 2021

DEDICATION

This book is dedicated to every single warrior soul, who at any point in their lives has or still is battling with themselves, with their minds, with their addictions and their pasts.

It is dedicated to all those who struggle to find and maintain connections worth their love due to reactions and survival instincts left over from unhealed traumas, instincts that have kept them alive through the most difficult and darkest of times.

Keep fighting warrior souls, I see you !

Special dedication to the Marvelous One, for without having met your beautiful expressive soul, this book would never have come to be.

This one's for you Sunshine , keep fighting x

PREFACE

I began on my writing journey about 6 months ago, as a way to ease my overthinking and negative thought patterns, a way to get the feelings out in situations I felt unable to speak in.
Upon being informed that actually my poems were pretty good, my confidence inflated.
I began making my words public on social media , and came upon a writing challenge...21 poems in 21 days. The result of the challenge? This book!!. Compiled of 21 soul speaking, colourfully emotional poems. A book of recognition to the inspiration of the warrior souls we have within. The first in what I hope to be a long line of books to come .

Breathtaking

Deep like the ocean,
Some souls know not of shallow waters.
For they were forged from the fires
Of the deepest volcano
On the darkest ocean floors.
Few see the beauty
In the depth of the warrior souls
Born this way
Screaming...into the world without so much
As a breath of oxygen to aid them.
Now that is strength
A beautiful iron like strength
So withstanding that the highest of waves
Could not crush it beneath its might.
This kind of strength intimidates those
That are used to a lesser soul,
A lesser strength,
A lesser depth,
A lesser love.
Wait for the one who recognises
The beauty of the fire burning behind your eyes,
Knows the depths from which it swam,
Yet still refuses to flinch in fear of your
magnificent intensity.
Do not dim your light for anyone,

For you are absolutely breathtaking.

Crazy mind, Crazy heart

Two crazy minds with two crazy hearts,
Two different lives with two different starts.
Both came with baggage and traumas unhealed,
The depth of which was soon to be revealed.
Without love what else is there? Shouldn't it be enough?
But for these two crazy hearts scared of love, it was tough.

Both ridden with guilt for imaginary crimes,
Intensified by the silent passing of time.
Scared to project to the other their hurts,
The guilt and the shame just made everything worse.
Now no one is speaking, the damage is done,
The battle is over but nobody won.
Boundaries were crossed , words said in haste,
This amazing connection was thrown to the waste.

Two broken minds with two broken hearts.
Two broken lives from two broken starts.

Match of
Absolution

There are many different reasons
Behind the bridges that we burn
In the connections that we torch,
destructive behaviours that we learned.
The shame and the resentments
Dark secrets that we hold
Real fears of hurting loved ones
With sins that go untold

If only we could see the light
Through this putrid smelling smoke
Our crazy brains and beautiful minds
Might not feel quite so broke
Alas we can not see the way
Through the fog that gathers now...

Striking a match of absolution
We burn it to the ground

I See You

I see you standing there.
Holding the weight of the world on your
shoulders,
Trying desperately to not get crushed under the
ever growing boulder you carry.

Board up that broken heart my love
Keep every last piece safe,
In your fortress with its watchtowers
Behind those steely gates.
Those masterful defenses
Keeping everyone at bay
Attacks dogs at the entrance
Keeping everyone away.
You think your on your own now,
No one's coming to save the day.
Little do you realise
I'm with you all the way.
Until that heart is mended
and the Marvelous returns,
Il watch you fighting battles,
holding pieces, catching burns.
I can not help you fight this war
And you wouldn't want me too
So I sit here with my pieces I protected

Just like you

Masquerade

How long can you go on pretending,
that you feel no pain?
No signs of any turmoil ,
any worry , any strain
Can you really shut everyone and everything
out?
All the hurt, disappointment,
the loss and the doubt?
Or
When your at home all
alone in your bed,
Do the thoughts and emotions
twist round in your head?
The remedies for your memories,
are they really all they seem?
Or is it just a masquerade so your pain can not
be seen...

Drawn

I've always been drawn to broken hearts and
warrior souls,
Those that have fallen and got back up a
thousand times before.
The ones who continuously battle to make sense
of the hand they were dealt
When choices weren't a luxury that was ever
freely given out.
Beautiful battle hardened beings who have hit
the hard rocky ground, had picnics with their
demons within,
then called it a night when they missed the
feeling,
of seeing the sunrise and warmth it brings to
their soul.
Soldiers of life, of love, of mind, that have found
ways to survive no matter how destructive to
self it may seem to the rest of the world.
You're still here, you're still surviving,
I see your strength,
It is astounding.

Hidden Light

I can feel in your words
That your light has gone out.
The magic you hold inside
Hiding like a secret
In a dark protected space
Just waiting until
You realise you have use for it once again
You may not feel
Much like magic right now
But my darling Lost Boy
Even in your darkness

You are Magic.

Your light will resurface again
When you are ready
With an explosion so intense

You will burn bright with all the colours of the
most spectacular supernova!

Musical Silence

Even though there may be distance
We will never be apart
Even through this silence
You play music in my heart
An octave of emotions
An orchestra of light
A confidence in my expression
That will carry through the night
Know that if we never speak again
I will forever hold you dear
Hearing your sweet symphonies
Play gently in my ear

A Life Half Lived

Walking through life,
Seeing the world go by
As if through a pane of imaginary glass.
Separating from all real connection.
There, but not really there.
A ghost haunting a once lived life,
void now of any direction or purpose you once
knew.
That was stolen, decades ago,
and now your left trying to survive
Without the knowledge or the know how,
of how to reconnect
with what you once loved,
of how to reconstruct yourself
having been wandering in the mist directionless.
A broken compass
Your only hope of finding your way back,
Refuses to point to any direction
Other than to the bottom of a bag full of poison.
It's effects numbing the emptiness
that has made a home inside of your soul for
what feels like an eternity.
Little distraction is the chemically induced
sociability that you hide behind.

You deserve to experience the world in all its
magnificent glory.
Bath in the love that each and every one of us
deserves

You deserve so much more
Than you ever thought you did
Believe it beautiful soul,
You deserve to live

Duality Of Mind

The duality of my ever warring mind
Consisting of two factions
Painfully intertwined
One side fights for love and light
And hope in all things dark
Setting my soul on fire
Bringing warmth to an empty heart.

The other leads the way for destruction
And the pain
Forgetting we all have battles
And are warring through the rain.
Drenched in doubts of how others feel
Consumed,they are too kind
To tell me my heart is too broken
My body too defiled

The fear of being pitied for the traumas
I've endured
That others might leave
Save having to witness my destruction
with no available cure

I know not how long this battle
Will rage this time around

But I stand tall
With the light I have within
However currently small
Once again victorious
This light it will survive
I refuse to let this part of me
be forced to run and hide

You Got A Mention

Someone mentioned you today.
It's seems no matter how much time goes by
that feeling never really goes away.
The little sting to my heart as it skips a couple of
beats. Regardless of how hard I try, my heart
will never admit defeat.
I hear you are still a warrior fighting battles in
your head. I hope the many demons that are
laying up ahead
Won't be too fierce a challenge on this long and
weary night,
with battle armour damaged
Don't you dare give up the fight
You have a long journey through this war torn
no mans land
But with a fire in your heart, you wield a
strength that can truly withstand.
I hope one day you return victorious
To the sounds of the marching band

Tsunami of the Mind

A vast ocean of feelings, and thoughts you hold
at bay. Waves topped with crests of pure
emotion, riding all the way.
A tidal wave of substances, you used to keep
you safe, won't hold off the tsunami about to
decimate this place.
If only you felt safe enough to face these fears
head on. Ending this weary battle that's been
raging for so long.
The only way to finally win, is to go deep inside,
face those feelings and emotions that you have
always tried to hide.
For once you open up the gates and let the water
in, eventually flowing out again, taking your
guilt and imaginary sin.
As you survey the wreckage and the debris left
behind, gathering the pieces that are left inside
your mind. The voice of repressed expression, to
your shores no longer tied.

Instead a lighthouse stands there,
shining out to sea.

Calming waters bring a blissful peace that was
always meant to be.
No more raging undercurrents,
no more need to self destruct
Allow your soul to speak its truth
Allow your heart to love

You Don't Know Me

One of those events, I'm sure you know the ones
Where every member of your family inevitably
comes.
Gran with her china cup of tea, uncles, aunties,
mums. Cousins, sisters , Grandad, don't forget
the sons.
They all say "hi" and "how are you" and the
boring "nice to see you too"
That's where it ends, there is no more to see,
I don't really know these people, and they
certainly don't know me.
I went into care, where were you then,with the
things I endured again and again?
You all left me alone, no attempt to connect,or
come to the rescue, my walls now erect.
Standing there talking , in your little groups,
laughing at old stories, showing photos too.
I can't relate to any of this, I know you see it too.
I have never felt so lonely as when I'm with all
of you

Expressionally Free

Although our love may not have had
Chance to make a stay
Truth be told you touched my soul
In a Spectacular kind of way
I had this pain inside of me
For which there was no cure
Until you opened up a side to me
Expresionally pure
I always had a love for words
And a love for poetry
But never did I dream
Such emotion penned by me
Like a light had been switched on
In my overcrowded head
Now I put pen to paper
And I write it out instead
The realisation that this gift
Could help me get ahead
Finally able to rid myself
Of this internal dread
The eggshells for others
That I now refuse to tread
And allow myself to stop
The tears I have continuously bled.
Now the words of my emotions

Finally are free
Flowing smoothly, serenely
With ease out of me
As the tide goes out with the
Deep calming sea
No more currents of torment
And unspoken words
To pull me back into that
Unspoken world

Now I find myself poetically free
To express my complexities
That no one has seen
They will never know how
This feels for me

To be fully, completely expressively free

Kaleidoscopes and Tiny Pieces

Kaleidoscopes are structures
Holding tiny broken pieces
Peering through you see
All the beauty it releases
With its layers of many colours
Penetrative, iris pleasing
As I gaze upon this sight
Multicoloured rays of light
My anxiety is easing
And I think that your the reason
A beauty like no other
Broken soul that I've encountered
Even though vast distance wandered
Through this ever barren land
This encounter had its reason
My imagination woken
The linguistic flow unbroken
I'm now solid where I stand
The gift of writing given
Now expressing things kept hidden
From my ever warring mind
Now the poetry is flowing

With the healing its bestowing
And the knowledge ever knowing
How to halt the ever bowing
To this storm continuously raging
Forever on inside

Now I feel a sense of calmness
This gift that I now harness
Will stay with me regardless
Of you going with the tide

That kaleidoscope of beauty
And it's tiny broken bits
Changed me so acutely
In some ways that really hit

 I hope your light is shining bright
As you travel through the night
Holding your lantern tightly
You will always be alright
Should you ever choose to visit
And so once again allow
To see the beauty you keep hidden
From those who gather round your prison
Wanting explanations given
For the changes that have risen
From the learning of hard lessons.
There is nothing that's more freeing
Than the feeling of releasing

All that pent up self expression

Let it out!

Abandonment Issues

When you leave and the abandonment issues
kick in, panic grips my chest with shallow
breathing.
Then the impulse to fix it builds from within, as
my nerves start to wear incredibly thin.
My logical brain then throws in the towel,
trauma brain takes the stage...this could go on
for hours.
Fighting hard with myself losing impulse
control,
"Just talk to someone" I'm forever being told.
But guess what happens when my fears are
divulged.

It's not your fault, you didn't do this to me, these
jagged edges of mine, I allowed you to see.
These historical wounds that won't let me be
free, are not your doing, please don't think you
broke me.

I understand needing space is not an attack

Trust it gets easier, because every time you come back

Except this time...

I'll Wait Right Here

I'll wait right here...

I know you are still searching for something you haven't found yet. Still turning over those rocks within, still learning of the things you are made of. Excavating and discovering the things in yourself that you admire.
So go, find those wondrous treasures, residing on your own sandy shaws, fighting and scraping your way through the dirt and the mess inside.
Fall in and out of love, breaking your own heart in the process with absolutely no fear, feel the sting of giving up on your biggest dreams.
Do not be afraid or ashamed to change direction whilst following the compass of your own heart.
Just please...never settle

Promise me you will never wed to the society of normals that do not know what it is to truly feel.

I will not trail you however, I refuse to beat anyone around the head with the depths of my heart.

I know love can be all about timing, and
currently we are but two wheels that just can not
turn in unison.
Both on our own journeys of discovery, although
I'm a little further along.

I will wait right here...
And when you find what it is you have been
searching for inside yourself for all this time,
Bring it to me, please.
Let me show you how I always saw these things
in you, long before you could see them in
yourself.

Maybe then
The time will be right for us to finally exist

Words Left Unsaid

It's a defense mechanism the way you shut
people out.
The ones you know are capable of bringing
change about.
You sit there in your comfort zone hiding from
the truth
Blocking out the pain of your resistance to your
growth.
Do you think by cutting off the ones who want
to see you win
You can hold off all the growing pains you
harbour deep within
You do yourself a hardship with those you
choose to be around
The toxic kind of friendships that forever hold
you down
Those that help enable you to stay sitting in the
dark
Only seem to drain your light to fix their own
broken hearts
I hope one day you see this and decide to leave
the night
Stop fighting off your growth and head into the
light

I wish for you that you find peace from all inside
your head
A place where you feel safe enough to express
all you left unsaid

Ode to my Daughter

Look at you now, almost 15years old,
How in this world could I make such a perfect
soul
You will never understand how you changed my
chaotic life from one of desperation to full of
hope, overnight
Angel by name, Angel by nature, the name
couldn't be more right
Because you never fail to guide me with your
love through out the night
My life was but an empty shell before you came
along
But when I found I was with child, the love
inside grew strong
The damage that was done to me, would never
be done to you
For I will protect you with my life until my days
are through
I can not express enough how proud of you I've
come to be
Without a doubt the very best thing to ever come
from me

Still Bleeding

We moved on, decided it was what was best,
Rather than destroy each other by loving in
ways neither one of us felt we deserved.
So why...when we went to the heartbreaking
efforts of sealing our love in an unbreakable
box, lost to the depths
Why ... if it was indeed what was best, even after
all this time apart
Why do our hearts and souls still bleed for one
another?

Letter to a Lost Boy

Lost boy, where have you gone?
Are you safe where you are, hidden up there in
your fortress of fear?
I wonder sometimes if you will ever make it
down from that tower up high,
High enough that even the most skilled of
archers could not dream to penetrate what is left
of that broken heart you protect.
Be not afraid of my beautiful warrior soul, for
there is no one left to fight.
Except those demons that you keep as pets,
Caged up inside your mind.
I will not lose hope, and continue to hold space
for a day such as when,
The weary soldier lays down his weapons, and
sees his worth again.
Lost Boy, when you decide that it is time, that
the darkness can no longer contain you,
When you realise that your crazy mind and
beautiful heart has a purpose, and that you are
ready to not be lost anymore...
I will guide you out, as my own soul mirrors
yours.
Reflecting the light that you
Could not,would not

See in yourself for so long.
Come back Lost Boy

It's time...